THE WORLD OF MARTIAL ARTS
GRAPPLING

BY JIM OLLHOFF

Published by ABDO Publishing Company, 8000 West 78th Street, Suite 310, Edina, MN 55439.
Copyright ©2008 by Abdo Consulting Group, Inc. International copyrights reserved in all countries.
No part of this book may be reproduced in any form without written permission from the publisher.
ABDO & Daughters™ is a trademark and logo of ABDO Publishing Company.

Printed in the United States.

Editor: John Hamilton
Graphic Design: John Hamilton
Cover Design: Neil Klinepier
Cover Illustration: Getty Images
Interior Photos and Illustrations: p 1 judo throw, Getty Images; p 5 judo throw, Getty Images; p 7 small woman throwing man, Getty Images; p 8 arm bar and throw, iStockphoto; p 9 arm bar, iStockphoto; p 11 judo flip, Getty Images; p 12 judo throw, Getty Images; p 13 arm throw, iStockphoto; p 15 girl puts boy in headlock, iStockphoto; p 16 Dr. Jigoro Kano, Corbis; p 17 men practicing judo on beach, iStockphoto; p 18 judo competitors at Athens Olympics, Getty Images; p 19 breakfall, iStockphoto; p 20, Morihei Ueshiba, courtesy Aikido Center of Miami; p 21 aikido stylists practice breakfalls, Corbis; p 22 aikido chin push, Corbis; p 23 aikido arm bar, Corbis; p 25 jiu-jitsu arm bar, iStockphoto; p 26 headlock, Getty Images; p 27 jiu-jitsu head strike, Getty Images; p 28 jiu-jitsu joint lock, Getty Images; p 29 Royce Gracie competing, Getty Images; p 31 arm grabs, iStockphoto.

Library of Congress Cataloging-in-Publication Data

Ollhoff, Jim, 1959-
  Grappling / Jim Ollhoff.
      p. cm. -- (The world of martial arts)
  Includes index.
  ISBN 978-1-59928-976-2
  1. Hand-to-hand fighting, Oriental--Juvenile literature. 2. Jiu-jitsu--Juvenile literature. 3. Self-defense--Juvenile literature. I. Title.

GV1112.O55 2008
796.81--dc22
                        2007030546

CONTENTS

THE GRAPPLING ARTS

Some martial arts emphasize kicking, like Korean tae kwon do. Other martial arts use strong punches from a wide stance, like karate from Japan or Okinawa. Some martial arts emphasize speed, like Chinese kung fu. Some emphasize deception and acrobatics, like Brazilian capoeira.

However, there are a few martial arts that emphasize grappling. Grappling means to grab and then manipulate an opponent's body. It teaches how to move in close and throw an opponent to the ground, or how to hold and twist someone's arm or leg to cause pain. Grappling uses the science of leverage. That means even a small or weak person can win a fight using the proper techniques.

Grappling, like all martial arts, should be defensive. Grappling arts should never be used to attack, only to defend.

Several martial arts styles emphasize grappling. This book will discuss three popular styles: judo, aikido, and Brazilian jiu-jitsu.

Facing page: A martial artist executes a judo throw against his opponent. Judo is one of several martial arts that emphasize grappling. Grappling uses the science of leverage to overcome attackers.

THE POWER OF LEVERAGE

How can a small person throw a big person? That question can be answered with one word: leverage. Imagine a muscular, 250-pound (113 kg) college football player. Could a seventh-grade girl push him over? Probably not. No matter how hard the girl pushes, the football player stays steady on his feet because he weighs so much more than she does. Even if he starts to tip, he can adjust his feet and push back against her.

But what if the football player is forced to stand on one foot on top of a small soup can? Could the seventh-grader push him off? Of course! In this case, the football player has no leverage. It would be easy to push him off, no matter how much he weighed.

That's the principle of the grappling arts. It doesn't matter how much an opponent weighs, or whether an opponent is tall or short. Leverage is the thing that matters. If a small person can move to get a leverage advantage, then a small person can easily throw a large person.

Facing page: The secret of grappling is leverage, which allows even small martial artists to overcome large opponents.

There are many stories of elderly judo stylists who demonstrate their skills. These 80-year-old men can throw 250-pound (113 kg) football players as if they were poker chips. They can do this because they understand the principles of leverage.

So, leverage is the most important skill in grappling. It doesn't matter if an opponent is big or small—the person with leverage will have a big advantage. The grappling arts teach the skill of gaining leverage.

Here's another way to look at it: can you lift your teacher 6 feet (1.8 m) off the ground? Probably not. But what if your teacher were sitting on a teeter-totter on the playground? If you were pressing down on the other side of the board, then you probably could lift your teacher off the ground. That's another example of leverage. Weight, height, and strength do not matter as much if you have leverage.

Below: A judo stylist puts his opponent in an arm bar and then tosses him to the mat.

Leverage allows a martial artist to apply the minimum force needed to get maximum results. Imagine putting an opponent in an arm bar, with the arm behind and wrist bent upward. At this point, you have control over your opponent's entire body, just by holding the wrist. You can make the opponent drop to the ground by applying pressure to the wrist and elbow. You can force the opponent to walk by pushing forward and applying a small amount of pressure. You have leverage on your opponent's arm, so you control his or her entire body.

Below: By applying the proper amount of leverage in a joint lock, an opponent can be subdued and controlled with even a small amount of pressure.

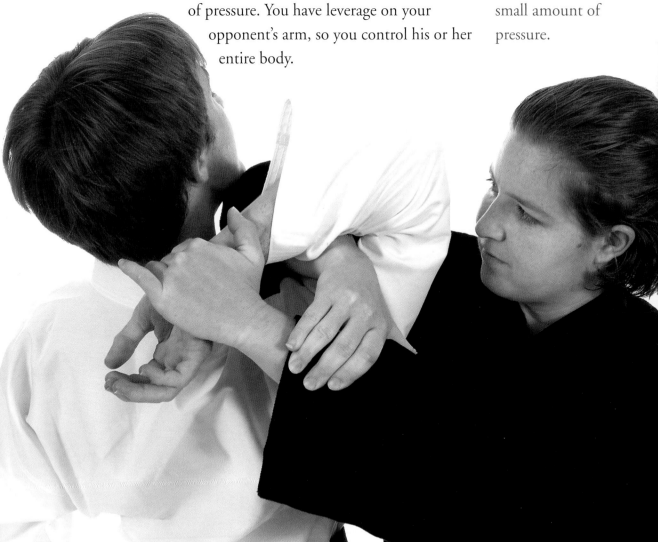

The Science of Weight and Momentum

Another way to understand leverage is to take advantage of an opponent's weight and momentum. This is one of the principles of the grappling arts: use your opponents' own weight and momentum against them. For example, pretend an attacker is running toward you. The attacker's weight moves forward, providing lots of momentum. If you stand still, the attacker will crash into you.

But instead of just standing still, what would happen if you moved backwards? What if you moved a little faster than your attacker? You would have time to grab the attacker and pull forward, causing your opponent to lose balance.

Or, instead of stepping back, what if you stepped to one side? You could push the attacker on the back as he ran by, causing him to go unexpectedly faster. There's a good chance the attacker will lose his balance and fall down.

What if you stepped to one side and put out your arm, pressing it against the attacker's neck or head in a clothesline defense? Momentum carries the attacker's body forward, but his head stays in one place. The attacker's feet fly up, causing him to land flat on his back.

Facing page: Martial artists train to use their opponents' own weight and momentum against them, often with high-flying results.

10

Below: By changing an opponent's direction of motion, a martial artist can easily stop an attack and toss the opponent to the floor.

These types of defenses are called "controlling your attacker by leading the attack." A grappling master subtly changes an attacker's direction of motion. By controlling direction, the attack is weakened.

The grappling arts are not about brute strength. Instead, they emphasize finesse, skill, and flexibility. The grappling arts teach how to control an opponent's weight and momentum. When a grappler controls leverage and momentum, an attacker becomes helpless.

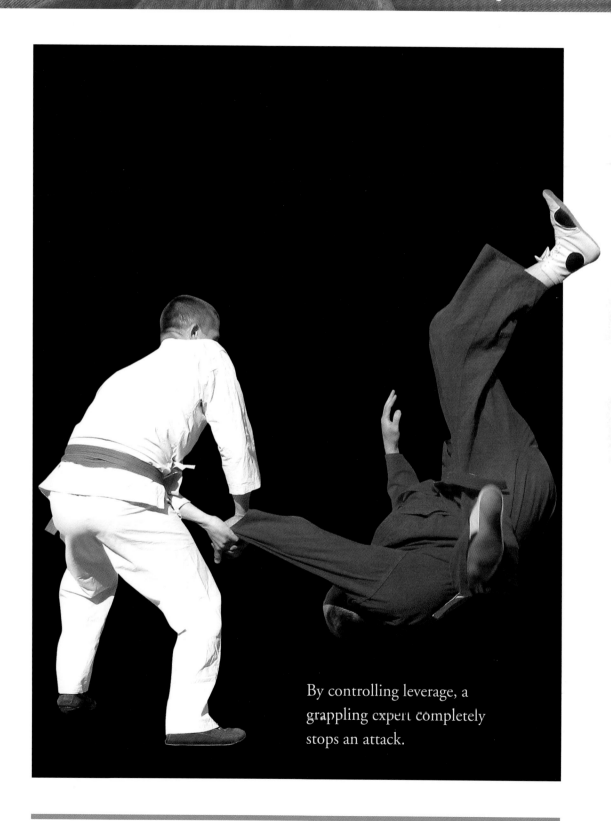

By controlling leverage, a grappling expert completely stops an attack.

Learning How to Use Control

A big part of grappling is learning how to use control. Control means using the right amount of force instead of too much force. In some styles, the martial artist tries to use as much force as possible when throwing a punch or kick. In grappling, the martial artist must be careful not to use full force, only enough to get the job done. Sometimes a technique needs only a little amount of force. Other times, a medium amount is required. The important thing is to know how much force to use for each technique.

This is especially true when practicing with other students. For example, if you are sparring with a friend at a Brazilian jiu-jitsu school, you might put him or her in an arm lock. If you use too much force in a joint lock, you could break or severely injure your partner. Brazilian jiu-jitsu stylists need to understand how much force to use in every situation.

Learning to grapple means learning how the body works. One must know how each joint bends, and how to manipulate it to get an advantage over an attacker. One must learn about balance, leverage, weight, and momentum. One must also learn to make fast choices in order to take advantage of an opponent's mistake.

Right: The use of proper control to avoid injury is very important when practicing martial arts.

JUDO

The story of judo began on October 28, 1860, with the birth of its founder, Dr. Jigoro Kano. He was born in the seaside town of Mikage in Japan. His family moved to Tokyo when he was a young child.

As a boy, Kano was small and frail, and sick much of the time. Bullies harassed him frequently because of his small size. He wanted to become more fit and healthy, but couldn't. Things started to change for him when he turned 18 years old. He went off to college to study literature. Kano also began studying martial arts.

Below: Dr. Jigoro Kano, the founder of judo.

In Japan in the late 1800s, there was a popular martial art called *jujitsu.* Samurai warriors used this traditional unarmed fighting style, which consisted of punches, kicks, and grapples. Kano studied several different schools of jujitsu. He realized that all the different schools had their strengths and weaknesses. He practiced what he believed to be the best of all the schools, took out some of the more dangerous techniques, and in 1882 opened his first school. He called his style *judo*, which means "the gentle way." He believed his martial art was the gentle way to learn about life.

Left: Two martial artists practice judo throws on a beach.

His first school only had a few students, but it quickly grew in popularity. Soon, a rivalry developed between the jujitsu and judo schools. With the help of the Tokyo police, the two rivals organized a tournament. Each school sent 15 men. The judo students won 13 matches. The other two matches were tied. Judo's popularity skyrocketed. Kano continued to refine judo. He also demanded that his students have high ethical standards. Judo students had to be considerate of others, make good moral decisions, and be interested in helping other students learn.

Above: Two judo stylists compete at the 2004 Summer Olympic Games in Athens, Greece.

Later, Kano received his doctorate degree and began teaching at a university. He became an important educator in Japan. However, he never stopped teaching judo. He made several trips to the United States. One of his students even demonstrated judo to President Theodore Roosevelt. During the 1930s, judo schools began to appear in the United States.

Dr. Kano died of pneumonia in May 1938, while returning from the Cairo International Olympic Conference. He was 78 years old.

Today, judo is both a martial art and a sport. Men's judo was first included in the Olympic Games in 1964, which was a fulfillment of Dr. Kano's dream. In 1992, women's judo became part of the Olympic Games as well.

Two judo contestants begin a match by grabbing each other's uniform. With one hand, they grab the collar, and with the other hand, they hold the sleeve of the uniform near the elbow. Then, they maneuver their legs and hips and upper body until one has the advantage. The goal is for one contestant to throw the other to the ground.

The first thing new students learn is how to fall. Because judo is filled with throws, trips, and falls, students need to know how to fall without hurting themselves. If the arm is in the wrong place in a fall, the elbow or shoulder can sustain painful injury. The correct way to fall, just like learning judo itself, should be taught by a trained instructor.

Left: In order to avoid injury, one of the first things a grappling stylist must learn is how to fall properly.

AIKIDO

Aikido is a Japanese martial art that was created in the early twentieth century. It is a graceful art that uses leverage to subdue an opponent without harm.

The word *aikido* comes from a Japanese word that describes a process of "moving together" in rhythm. The aikido stylist moves together with the attacker so that the attacker can be subdued. Aikido teaches throws and movements that will subdue but not harm the attacker. Other martial arts emphasize brute force with punches and kicks. Aikido is different. In aikido, the martial artist uses a small amount of force to subdue an attacker.

The founder of aikido, Morihei Ueshiba, believed that its purpose is to show love and compassion to all people, even those who would try to harm you. Aikido masters believe that if you are attacked, you should defend yourself, but without hurting or maiming the attacker. The attacker is behaving at a lower level, without thinking, almost as an animal would behave.

However, if you are an aikido stylist, you have better confidence than an attacker, a better way of behaving, and a better sense of right and wrong. It is the aikido stylist's responsibility not to inflict unnecessary damage on an attacker.

Below: Morihei Ueshiba, the founder of aikido.

Above: Two aikido stylists practice self-defense techniques.

Above: Aikido emphasizes circular motions to gain leverage on attackers.

Morihei Ueshiba, the founder of aikido, was born in the Japanese city of Tanabe in 1883. His grandfather had been a samurai. In his youth, Ueshiba studied sumo, jujitsu, aiki-jujitsu, and judo.

In the 1920s and 1930s, Ueshiba developed his own martial art. Instead of strikes, such as punches and kicks, he concentrated on throws and joint locks. Ueshiba placed more emphasis on circular motion and moving the whole body in order to gain maximum leverage on an attacker. Aikido teaches how to use an opponent's own weight and momentum to stop an attack.

Ueshiba was a deeply religious man. He thought constantly about how to create peace in the world. During the worst of the fighting in World War II, Ueshiba wrote, "To smash, injure, or destroy is the worst sin a human being can commit. The real Way of the Warrior is to prevent slaughter." He taught aikido as a way to create peace in the world. In fact, he often referred to aikido as the "art of peace."

As with many martial arts, one of the first things students learn is how to fall correctly in order to prevent injury. As they fall, students reach out and slap the ground with their hand, which deflects some of the impact. This is called a "breakfall."

Aikido students learn how to move quickly and gracefully. They observe an opponent's momentum and learn how to change it very slightly, sometimes with just a light touch, so that the opponent loses balance and falls. Students also learn how to grab and manipulate wrists, elbows, and other body parts so that they can subdue, rather than harm, an attacker.

Ueshiba declared, "To injure your opponent is to injure yourself. To control aggression without inflicting injury is the Art of Peace." That is the essence of the martial art he founded. Aikido seeks to control aggression without inflicting injury. Ueshiba died in 1969, leaving behind many devoted students and a popular, thriving martial art.

Below: An aikido stylist puts an opponent into a joint lock.

BRAZILIAN JIU-JITSU

Brazilian jiu-jitsu is a popular grappling art that emphasizes ground fighting. One of its main ideas is that a smaller person can subdue a bigger, stronger opponent while they are on the ground.

Mitsuyo Maeda was born in Japan in 1878. As a teenager, he began to practice sumo, but decided it was not for him. When he went off to college in Tokyo, he took up the study of judo from its founder, Jigoro Kano. After becoming an expert in judo, Maeda traveled widely. He traveled to Europe, the United States, and Central America. He fought in many exhibition matches and became a professional fighter. By 1917, he had settled in Brazil. There, he moved from being a professional fighter to being a teacher.

Maeda called his art *jujitsu*. Maeda's teacher, Jigoro Kano, worked hard to make clear the distinction between judo and jujitsu. However, outside of Japan, many people thought the two styles were the same. It's not clear why Mitsuyo Maeda called his style jujitsu. It might be that he called the style jujitsu because, at that time, it was a better-known term.

Left: A jiu-jitsu stylist subdues an opponent with an arm bar.

Above: A black belt martial artist puts an opponent into a headlock and prepares to flip her to the ground.

One day in 1917, a 14-year-old boy named Carlos Gracie watched a demonstration by Maeda. He decided to learn this new art, and became a student of Maeda.

After several years of study, Carlos and his family moved to Rio de Janeiro, Brazil. Carlos passed the new fighting techniques on to his brothers and his children.

One of Carlos' brothers, Helio Gracie, was at first too sick to take part in the practice sessions. However, Helio watched carefully, and eventually overcame his health problems. When he began to do the techniques, he found they were difficult for him. He was smaller and weaker than many of his brothers. Helio paid careful attention to using leverage rather than brute strength. He learned how to grab, grapple, and hold so that his small size wasn't a disadvantage.

As time went on, Helio Gracie became a master of these techniques. He became the founder of the style known as *Brazilian jiu-jitsu*, or more specifically, *Gracie jiu-jitsu*.

Brazilian jiu-jitsu artists like to "take the fight to the ground." They are much more comfortable fighting on the ground than standing up. While they are on the ground, Brazilian jiu-jitsu stylists can use their legs and feet as well as their hands. This gives them many more weapons. Brazilian jiu-jitsu stylists like to say that in real life, most fights end up on the ground. Therefore, they say, their style is particularly effective. It's true that fights often end up on the ground, especially when the fight lasts a long time. Brazilian jiu-jitsu is very effective on the ground when fighting a single opponent.

Below: A martial artist demonstrates a jiu-jitsu strike to the head.

Above: A jiu-jitsu stylist puts her opponent into a joint lock.

The popularity of the sport grew, and rules for tournaments were developed. The matches were usually won by submissions. A submission is when an opponent surrenders by tapping the mat with his or her hand. This is called "tapping out." Submissions usually occur when the victor puts the loser in a joint lock or choke. A joint lock is a position where a part of the body is bent unnaturally, and the pain of the joint lock makes the loser tap out. A chokehold occurs when the loser can't breathe, or loses blood circulation to the head.

Brazilian jiu-jitsu became famous across the world in the early 1990s. One of Helio Gracie's sons, Rorion Gracie, was looking for a place to showcase his father's martial art. Rorion Gracie and some others founded a tournament called the Ultimate Fighting Championship. They designed it as a forum where practitioners of different martial arts could come together to fight.

The Ultimate Fighting Championship was a televised series of matches in which two martial artists fought until one tapped out, or until the referee stopped the fight. Referees sometimes stopped a fight because a competitor could no longer defend himself.

Ultimate Fighting Championship matches were billed as "mixed martial arts," where opponents could use any technique from any style they wanted. Promoters liked to proclaim that "there are no rules" in mixed martial arts, which of course wasn't true. However, it gave an excitement to the fights. That excitement caught on quickly, and mixed martial arts tournaments became very popular.

Another one of Helio Gracie's sons, Royce Gracie, was selected to fight in the first Ultimate Fighting Championship. Royce won the tournament. Royce Gracie also won the second and fourth Ultimate Fighting Championship tournaments. Because the Ultimate Fighting Championship was very popular, Brazilian jiu-jitsu suddenly became famous. Brazilian jiu-jitsu continues to be a popular martial art and an exciting sport to watch.

Below: Royce Gracie, in the white uniform, competes in an Ultimate Fighting Championship match.

GLOSSARY

Arm bar

An arm bar is a kind of joint lock in which the attacker's arm is leveraged and held straight, painfully flexing the elbow joint, and sometimes the shoulder joint. Arm bars are a common submission technique used in jiu-jitsu.

Belt

Most modern martial arts schools use a system of colored belts to rank their students based on their abilities and length of training. Each school decides the exact order of belts, but most are similar in ranking. A typical school might start beginner students at white belt. From there, the students progress to gold belt, then green, purple, blue, red, and brown. The highest belt is black. It usually takes from three to five years of intense training to achieve a black belt.

Capoeira

A martial art brought to Brazil by African slaves sometime in the early 1600s. Capoeira stylists are in constant motion, performing handstands, headspins, cartwheels, flips, and head butts.

Joint lock

A submission technique, often used in jiu-jitsu, judo, and aikido, in which an attacker's arm or leg is twisted and held tight so that a joint, such as an elbow, knee, or ankle, is painfully overextended.

Kung Fu

A Chinese martial art that had an early influence on the development of other martial arts worldwide, such as karate. The phrase *kung fu* means "achievement through great effort."

Okinawa

The birthplace of modern karate. The main island of Okinawa is part of the Ryukyu chain of islands, which are situated in the Pacific Ocean south of Japan. Although it was once an independent nation, Okinawa today is a prefecture, or state, of Japan.

Samurai

The trained warrior class of medieval Japan.

Tae Kwon Do

A hard-style form of martial arts that originated from Korea. Tae kwon do is known for its powerful kicks. The phrase *tae kwon do* means "the way of kicking and punching."

Tapping Out

During a martial arts match that involves grappling, when one fighter is being choked or is in intense pain, such as from a joint lock, he or she taps the mat with a hand. The referee immediately stops the fight. A smart fighter knows when to tap out: he loses the fight, but prevents injury.

Left: Two judo stylists prepare to compete by first gripping each other's uniform.

INDEX